The Plan of a Dictionary of the English Language; Addressed to the Right Honourable Philip Dormer, Earl of Chesterfield,

THE

P L A N

OF A

DICTIONARY

OF THE

ENGLISH LANGUAGE;

Addreſſed to the Right Honourable

PHILIP DORMER,

Earl of CHESTERFIELD,

One of His Majeſty's Principal Secretaries
of State.

LONDON·

Printed for J. and P. KNAPTON, T. LONGMAN and
T. SHEWELL, C HITCH, A MILLAR, and
R DODSLEY. MDCCXLVII

... to have been

... ...

... ...

My Lord,

WHEN firſt I undertook to write an Engliſh Dictionary, I had no expectation of any higher patronage than that of the proprietors of the copy, nor proſpect of any other advantage than the price of my labour; I knew, that the work in which I engaged is generally conſidered as drudgery for the blind, as the proper toil of artleſs induſtry, a taſk that requires neither the light of learning, nor the activity of genius, but may be ſuccefsfully performed without any higher quality than that of bearing burthens with dull patience, and beating the track of the alphabet with ſluggiſh reſolution.

WHETHER this opinion, ſo long tranſmitted and ſo widely propagated, had its beginning from truth and nature, or from accident and prejudice, whether it be decreed by the authority of reaſon, or the tyranny of ignorance, that of all the candidates for literary praiſe, the unhappy lexicographer

A holds

holds the lowest place, neither vanity nor interest incited me to enquire. It appeared that the province allotted me was of all the regions of learning generally confessed to be the least delightful, that it was believed to produce neither fruits nor flowers, and that after a long and laborious cultivation, not even the barren laurel had been found upon it.

YET on this province, my Lord, I enter'd with the pleasing hope, that as it was low, it likewise would be safe. I was drawn forward with the prospect of employment, which, tho' not splendid, would be useful, and which tho' it could not make my life envied, would keep it innocent, which would awaken no passion, engage me in no contention, nor throw in my way any temptation to disturb the quiet of others by censure, or my own by flattery.

I HAD read indeed of times, in which princes and statesmen thought it part of their honour to promote the improvement of their native tongues, and in which dictionaries were written under the protection of greatness. To the patrons of such undertakings, I willingly paid the homage of believing that they, who were thus solicitous for the perpetuity of their language, had reason to expect

that

that their actions would be celebrated by
posterity, and that the eloquence which they
promoted would be employed in their praise.
But I considered such acts of beneficence as
prodigies, recorded rather to raise wonder
than expectation; and content with the terms
that I had stipulated, had not suffer'd my imagination to flatter me with any other encou-
ragement, when I found that my design had
been thought by your Lordship of importance
sufficient to attract your favour.

How far this unexpected distinction can
be rated among the happy incidents of life,
I am not yet able to determine. Its first effect
has been to make me anxious lest it should fix
the attention of the public too much upon me,
and as it once happened to an epic poet of
France, by raising the reputation of the attempt, obstruct the reception of the work. I
imagine what the world will expect from a
scheme, prosecuted under your Lordship's in-
fluence, and I know that expectation, when
her wings are once expanded, easily reaches
heights which performance never will attain,
and when she has mounted the summit of perfection, derides her follower, who dies in the
pursuit.

Not

NOT therefore to raife expectation, but to reprefs it, I here lay before your Lordfhip the plan of my undertaking, that more may not be demanded than I intend, and that before it is too far advanced to be thrown into a new method, I may be advertifed of its defects or fuperfluities. Such informations I may juftly hope from the emulation with which thofe who defire the praife of elegance or difcernment muft contend in the promotion of a defign that you, my Lord, have not thought unworthy to fhare your attention with treaties and with wars.

IN the firft attempt to methodife my ideas, I found a difficulty which extended itfelf to the whole work. It was not eafy to determine by what rule of diftinction the words of this dictionary were to be chofen. The chief intent of it is to preferve the purity and afcertain the meaning of our Englifh idiom; and this feems to require nothing more than that our language be confidered fo far as it is our own, that the words and phrafes ufed in the general intercourfe of life, or found in the works of thofe whom we commonly ftile polite writers, be felected, without including the terms of particular profeffions, fince, with the arts to which they relate, they are generally derived from other nations, and are

4   very

very often the fame in all the languages of this part of the world. This is perhaps the exact and pure idea of a grammatical dictionary, but in lexicography, as in other arts, naked fcience is too delicate for the purpofes of life. The value of a work muft be eftimated by its ufe: it is not enough that a dictionary delights the critic, unlefs at the fame time it inftructs the learner; as it is to little purpofe, that an engine amufes the philofopher by the fubtilty of its mechanifm, if it requires fo much knowledge in its application, as to be of no advantage to the common workman.

THE title which I prefix to my work has long conveyed a very mifcellaneous idea, and they that take a dictionary into their hands have been accuftomed to expect from it, a folution of almoft every difficulty. If foreign words therefore were rejected, it could be little regarded, except by critics, or thofe who afpire to criticifm; and however it might enlighten thofe that write, would be all darknefs to them that only read The unlearned much oftner confult their dictionaries, for the meaning of words, than for their ftructures or formations, and the words that moft want explanation, are generally terms of art, which therefore experience has taught my predeceffors to fpread with a kind of pompous luxuriance over their productions. THE

The academicians of France, indeed, rejected terms of science in their firſt eſſay, but
found afterwards a neceſſity of relaxing the
rigour of their determination; and, though
they would not naturalize them at once by a
ſingle act, permitted them by degrees to ſettle
themſelves among the natives, with little oppoſition, and it would ſurely be no proof of
judgment to imitate them in an error which
they have now retracted, and deprive the book
of its chief uſe by ſcrupulous diſtinctions.

Of ſuch words however, all are not equally to be conſidered as parts of our language,
for ſome of them are naturalized and incorporated, but others ſtill continue aliens, and
are rather auxiliaries than ſubjects. This na-
turalization is produced either by an admiſ-
ſion into common ſpeech in ſome metaphorical ſignification, which is the acquiſition of a
kind of property among us, as we ſay the *ze-
nith* of advancement, the *meridian* of life, the
* *cynoſure* of neighbouring eyes; or it is the
conſequence of long intermixture and frequent
uſe, by which the ear is accuſtomed to the
ſound of words till their original is forgotten,
as in *equator*, *ſatellites*; or of the change of a
foreign to an Engliſh termination, and a conformity to the laws of the ſpeech into which
they

* Milton.

they are adopted, as in *category*, *cachexy*, *peripneumony*.

OF thofe which yet continue in the ftate of aliens, and have made no approaches towards affimilation, fome feem neceffary to be retained, becaufe the purchafers of the dictionary will expect to find them. Such are many words in the common law, as *capias*, *habeas corpus*, *præmunire*, *nifi prius* fuch are fome terms of controverfial divinity, as *hypoftafis*, and of phyfick, as the names of difeafes; and in general all terms which can be found in books not written profeffedly upon particular arts, or can be fuppofed neceffary to thofe who do not regularly ftudy them. Thus when a reader not fkilled in phyfick happens in Milton upon this line,

——————————— pining atrophy,
Marafmus, and wide-wafting peftilence.

he will with equal expectation look into his dictionary for the word *marafmus*, as for *atrophy*, or *peftilence*, and will have reafon to complain if he does not find it.

IT feems neceffary to the completion of a dictionary defigned not merely for critics but for popular ufe, that it fhould comprise, in fome degree, the peculiar words of every profeffion;

feſſion, that the terms of war and navigation ſhould be inſerted ſo far as they can be re-quired by readers of travels, and of hiſtory, and thoſe of law, merchandiſe and mechani-cal trades, ſo far as they can be ſuppoſed uſe-ful in the occurrences of common life.

But there ought, howevei, to be ſome di-ſtinction made between the different claſſes of words, and therefore it will be proper to print thoſe which are incorporated into the language in the uſual character, and thoſe which are ſtill to be conſidered as foreign in the Italick letter.

Another queſtion may ariſe, with regard to appellatives, or the names of ſpecies. It ſeems of no great uſe to ſet down the words *horſe, dog, cat, willow, alder, daſy, roſe,* and a thouſand others, of which it will be hard to give an explanation not more obſcure than the word itſelf. Yet it is to be conſidered, that, if the names of animals be inſerted, we muſt admit thoſe which are more known, as well as thoſe with which we are, by accident, leſs acquainted; and if they are all rejected, how will the reader be relieved from difficul-ties produced by alluſions to the crocodile, the camæleon, the ichneumon, and the hyæna? If no plants are to be mentioned, the moſt
pleaſing

pleafing part of nature will be excluded, and many beautiful epithets be unexplained. If only thofe which are lefs known are to be mentioned, who fhall fix the limits of the reader's learning? The importance of fuch explications appears from the miftakes which the want of them has occafioned. Had Shakefpear had a dictionary of this kind, he had not made the *woodbine* entwine the *honey-fuckle*; nor would Milton, with fuch affiftance, have difpofed fo improperly of his *ellops* and his *fcorpion*.

BESIDES, as fuch words, like others, require that their accents fhould be fettled, their founds afcertained, and their etymologies deduced, they cannot be properly omitted in the dictionary. And though the explanations of fome may be cenfured as trivial, becaufe they are almoft univerfally underftood, and thofe of others as unneceffary, becaufe they will feldom occur, yet it feems not proper to omit them, fince it is rather to be wifhed that many readers fhould find more than they expect, than that one fhould mifs what he might hope to find.

WHEN all the words are felected and arranged, the firft part of the work to be confidered is the ORTHOGRAPHY, which was long

vague

vague and uncertain, which at laft, when its fluctuation ceafed, was in many cafes fettled but by accident, and in which, according to your Lordfhip's obfervation, there is ftill great uncertainty among the beft critics, nor is it eafy to ftate a rule by which we may decide between cuftom and reafon, or between the equiponderant authorities of writers alike eminent for judgment and accuracy.

THE great orthographical conteft has long fubfifted between etymology and pronunciation. It has been demanded, on one hand, that men fhould write as they fpeak, but as it has been fhewn, that this conformity never was attained in any language, and that it is not more eafy to perfuade men to agree exactly in fpeaking than in writing, it may be afked with equal propriety, why men do not rather fpeak as they write In France, where this controverfy was at its greateft height, neither party, however ardent, durft adhere fteadily to their own rule; the etymologift was often forced to fpell with the people, and the advocate for the authority of pronunciation, found it fometimes deviating fo capricioufly from the received ufe of writing, that he was conftrained to comply with the rule of his adverfaries, left he fhould lofe the end by the

the means, and be left alone by following the
crowd.

WHEN a queſtion of orthography is dubi-
ous, that practice has, in my opinion, a claim
to preference, which preſerves the greateſt
number of radical letters, or ſeems moſt to
comply with the general cuſtom of our language. But the chief rule which I propoſe to
follow, is to make no innovation, without a
reaſon ſufficient to balance the inconvenience
of change, and ſuch reaſons I do not expect
often to find. All change is of itſelf an evil,
which ought not to be hazarded but for evi-
dent advantage, and as inconſtancy is in every
caſe a mark of weakneſs, it will add nothing
to the reputation of our tongue There are,
indeed, ſome who deſpiſe the inconveniencies
of confuſion, who ſeem to take pleaſure in
departing from cuſtom, and to think alteration deſirable for its own ſake, and the reformation of our orthography, which theſe writers have attempted, ſhould not paſs without
its due honours, but that I ſuppoſe they hold
ſingularity its own reward, or may dread the
faſcination of laviſh praiſe.

THE preſent uſage of ſpelling, where the preſent uſage can be diſtinguiſhed, will therefore
in this work be generally followed, yet there
B 2 will

will be often occasion to obferve, that it is in
itfelf inaccurate, and tolerated rather than
chofen, particularly, when by a change of
one letter, or more, the meaning of a word
is obfcured, as in *farrier*, for *ferrier*, as it was
formerly written, from *ferrum* or *fer*, in *gib-
berifh* for *geldifh*, the jargon of Geber and his
chymical followers, underftood by none but
their own tribe. It will be likewife fometimes
proper to trace back the orthography of different ages, and fhew by what gradations the
word departed from its original.

Closely connected with orthography is
Pronunciation, the ftability of which is of
great importance to the duration of a language, becaufe the firft change will naturally
begin by corruptions in the living fpeech.
The want of certain rules for the pronunciation of former ages, has made us wholly
ignorant of the metrical art of our ancient
poets; and fince thofe who ftudy their fenti-
ments regret the lofs of their numbers, it is
furely time to provide that the harmony of
the moderns may be more permanent.

A new pronounciation will make almoft
a new fpeech, and therefore fince one great
end of this undertaking is to fix the Englifh
language, care will be taken to determine the
accen-

accentuation of all polyfyllables by proper authorities, as it is one of thofe capricious phænomena which cannot be eafily reduced to rules. Thus there is no antecedent reafon for difference of accent in the two words *dolorous* and *fonorous*, yet of the one Milton gives the found in this line,

He pafs'd o'er many a region *dolorous*,

and that of the other in this,

Sonorous metal blowing martial founds.

IT may be likewife proper to remark metrical licences, fuch as contractions, *generous*, *gen'rous*, *reverend*, *rev'rend*; and coalitions, as *region*, *queftion*.

BUT it is ftill more neceffary to fix the pronunciation of monofyllables, by placing with them words of correfpondent found, that one may guard the other againft the danger of that variation, which to fome of the moft common has already happened, fo that the words *wound*, and *wind*, as they are now frequently pronounced, will not rhyme to *found*, and *mind* It is to be remarked that many words written alike are differently pronounc'd, as *flow*, and *brow*, which may be thus regiftred *flow*, *woe*, *brow*, *now*, or of which the exemplification may be generally given by a
distich.

diftich. Thus the words *tear* or lacerate, and
tear the water of the eye, have the fame letters, but may be diftinguifhed thus, *tear*,
dare, *tear*, *peer*.

SOME words have two founds, which may
be equally admitted, as being equally defen-
fible by authority. Thus *great* is differently
ufed.

For Swift and him defpis'd the faice of ftate,
The fober follies of the wife and *great*. POPE.

As if misfortune made the throne her feat,
And none could be unhappy but the *great*.
ROWE.

The care of fuch minute particulais may be
cenfured as trifling, but thefe particulars have
not been thought unworthy of attention in
more polifhed languages.

THE accuracy of the Fiench, in ftating the
founds of their letters, is well known; and,
among the Italians, Crefcembeni has not
thought it unneceffary to inform his country-
men of the woids, which, in compliance with
different ihymes, are allowed to be differently
fpelt, and of which the number is now fo
fixed, that no modern poet is fuffered to en-
creafe it.

7   WHEN

WHEN the orthography and pronunciation
are adjusted, the ETYMOLOGY or DERIVA-
TION is next to be considered, and the words
are to be distinguished according to their different classes, whether simple, as *day, light*, or
compound as *day-light*; whether primitive, as,
to *act*, or derivative, as *action, actionable, active,
activity*. This will much facilitate the attainment of our language, which now stands in
our dictionaries a confused heap of words
without dependence, and without relation.

WHEN this part of the work is performed,
it will be necessary to inquire how our pri-
mitives are to be deduced from foreign languages, which may be often very successfully
performed by the assistance of our own ety-
mologists. This search will give occasion to
many curious disquisitions, and sometimes
perhaps to conjectures, which, to readers un-
acquainted with this kind of study, cannot
but appear improbable and capricious. But
it may be reasonably imagined, that what is
so much in the power of men as language,
will very often be capriciously conducted.
Nor are these disquisitions and conjectures to
be considered altogether as wanton sports of
wit, or vain shews of learning, our language
is well known not to be primitive or self-ori-
ginated, but to have adopted words of every

genera-

generation, and either for the fupply of its necefſities, or the encreaſe of its copiouſneſs, to have received additions from very diſtant regions, ſo that in ſearch of the progenitors of our ſpeech, we may wander from the tropic to the frozen zone, and find ſome in the vallies of Paleſtine and ſome upon the rocks of Norway.

BESIDE the derivation of particular words, there is likewiſe an etymology of phraſes. Expreſſions are often taken from other languages, ſome apparently, as to *run a riſque, courir un riſque*, and ſome even when we do not ſeem to borrow their words, thus, to *bring about* or accompliſh, appears an Engliſh phraſe, but in reality our native word *about* has no ſuch import, and it is only a French expreſſion, of which we have an example in the common phraſe, *venir à bout d' une affaire*.

IN exhibiting the deſcent of our language, our etymologiſts ſeem to have been too laviſh of their learning, having traced almoſt every word through various tongues, only to ſhew what was ſhewn ſufficiently by the firſt derivation. This practice is of great uſe in ſynoptical lexicons, where mutilated and doubtful languages are explained by their affinity to others more certain and extenſive, but is gene-

geneially fuperfluous in Englifh etymologies.
When the woid is eafily deduced from a Saxon original, I fhall not often enquire fuither,
fince we know not the parent of the Saxon dialect, but when it is borrowed fiom the Fiench,
I fhall fhew whence the French is appaiently
derived. Where a Saxon root cannot be
found, the defect may be fupplied from kin-
dred languages, which will be generally fur-
nifhed with much liberality by the writers of
our gloffaries, writers who deferve often
the higheft praife, both of judgment and
induftry, and may expect at leaft to be mentioned with honoui by me, whom they have
freed fiom the greateft part of a very laborious work, and on whom they have impofed,
at woift, only the eafy tafk of rejecting fuperfluities.

By tiacing in this mannei eveiy word to its
oiiginal, and not admitting, but with gieat
caution, any of which no oiiginal can be
found, we fhall fecuie oui language fiom being over-iun with *cant*, fiom being ciouded
with low teims, the fpawn of folly oi affectation, which aiife fiom no juft piinciples of
fpeech, and of which therefoie no legitimate
deiivation can be fhewn

WHEN

WHEN the etymology is thus adjusted, the ANALOGY of our language is next to be considered, when we have discovered whence our words are derived, we are to examine by what rules they are governed, and how they are inflected through their various terminations. The terminations of the English are few, but those few have hitherto remained unregarded by the writers of our dictionaries. Our substantives are declined only by the plural termination, our adjectives admit no variation but in the degrees of comparison, and our verbs are conjugated by auxiliary words, and are only changed in the preter tense.

To our language may be with great justness applied the observation of *Quintilian*, that speech was not formed by an analogy sent from heaven. It did not descend to us in a state of uniformity and perfection, but was produced by necessity and enlarged by accident, and is therefore composed of dissimilar parts, thrown together by negligence, by affectation, by learning, or by ignorance.

OUR inflections therefore are by no means constant, but admit of numberless irregularities, which in this dictionary will be diligently noted. Thus *fox* makes in the plural *foxes*, but *ox* makes *oxen*. *Sheep* is the same in
both

both numbers. Adjectives are sometimes compared by changing the last syllable, as *proud, prouder, proudest*; and sometimes by particles prefixed, as *ambitious, more* ambitious, *most* ambitious. The forms of our verbs are subject to great variety, some end their preter tense in *ed*, as I *love*, I *loved*, I have *loved*, which may be called the regular form, and is followed by most of our verbs of southern original. But many depart from this rule, without agreeing in any other, as I *shake*, I *shook*, I have *shaken*, or *shook* as it is sometimes written in poetry; I *make*, I *made*, I have *made*; I *bring*, I *brought*, I *wring*, I *wrung*; and many others, which, as they cannot be reduced to rules, must be learned from the dictionary rather than the grammar.

THE verbs are likewise to be distinguished according to their qualities, as actives from neuters; the neglect of which has already introduced some barbarities in our conversation, which, if not obviated by just animadversions, may in time creep into our writings.

THUS, my Lord, will our language be laid down, distinct in its minutest subdivisions, and resolved into its elemental principles. And who upon this survey can forbear to wish, that these fundamental atoms of our speech

might

might obtain the firmnefs and immutability of the primogenial and conftituent particles of matter, that they might retain their fub-ftance while they alter their appearance, and be varied and compounded, yet not de-ftroyed.

But this is a privilege which words are fcarcely to expect, for, like their author, when they are not gaining ftrength, they are generally lofing it. Though art may fome-times prolong their duration, it will rarely give them perpetuity, and their changes will be almoft always informing us, that language is the work of man, of a being from whom permanence and ftability cannot be derived.

Words having been hitherto confidered as feparate and unconnected, are now to be likewife examined as they are ranged in their various relations to others by the rules of SYN-TAX or conftruction, to which I do not know that any regard has been yet fhewn in Englifh dictionaries, and in which the grammarians can give little affiftance The fyntax of this language is too inconftant to be reduced to rules, and can be only learned by the diftinct confideration of particular words as they are ufed by the beft authors. Thus, we fay according to the prefent modes of fpeech, the
foldier

foldier died *of* his wounds, and the failor pe-
rifhed *with* hunger, and every man acquainted with our language would be offended by a
change of thefe particles, which yet feem ori-
ginally affigned by chance, there being no reafon to be drawn from grammar why a man
may not, with equal propriety, be faid to dye
with a wound, or perifh *of* hunger.

Our fyntax therefore is not to be taught by
general rules, but by fpecial precedents; and
in examining whether Addifon has been with
juftice accufed of a folecifm in this paffage,

The poor inhabitant——
Starves in the midft of nature's bounty curft,
And in the loaden vineyard *dies for thirft,*

it is not in our power to have recourfe to any
eftablifhed laws of fpeech, but we muft remark how the writers of former ages have
ufed the fame word, and confider whether he
can be acquitted of impropriety, upon the
teftimony of Davies, given in his favour by
a fimilar paffage.

She loaths the watry glafs wherein fhe gaz'd,
And fhuns it ftill, although *for thirft fhe dye.*

When the conftruction of a word is explained, it is neceffary to purfue it through
its train of Phraseology, through thofe
forms

forms where it is ufed in a manner peculiar
to our language, or in fenfes not to be com-
prifed in the general explanations; as from
the verb *make*, arife thefe phrafes, to *make love*,
to *make an end*, to *make way*, as he *made way* for
his followers, the fhip *made way* before the
wind; to *make a bed*, to *make merry*, to *make
a mock*, to *make prefents*, to *make a doubt*, to
make out an affertion, to *make good* a breach,
to *make good* a caufe, to *make nothing* of an attempt, to *make lamentation*, to *make a merit*,
and many others which will occur in reading
with that view, and which only their frequency
hinders from being generally remarked.

THE great labour is yet to come, the labour of interpreting thefe words and phrafes
with brevity, fulnefs and perfpicuity; a tafk
of which the extent and intricacy is fuffici-
ently fhewn by the mifcarriage of thofe who
have generally attempted it. This difficulty
is increafed by the neceffity of explaining the
words in the fame language, for there is often
only one word for one idea; and though it
be eafy to tranflate the words *bright*, *fweet*,
falt, *bitter*, into another language, it is not
eafy to explain them.

WITH regard to the INTERPRETATION
many other queftions have required confideration.

tion. It was fome time doubted whether it be neceffary to explain the things implied by particular words. As under the term *baronet*, whether inftead of this explanation, *a title of honour next in degree to that of baron*, it would be better to mention more particularly the creation, privileges and rank of baronets ; and whether under the word *barometer*, inftead of being fatisfied with obferving that it is *an inftrument to difcover the weight of the air*, it would be fit to fpend a few lines upon its invention, conftruction and principles. It is not to be expected that with the explanation of the one the herald fhould be fatisfied, or the philofopher with that of the other ; but fince it will be required by common readers, that the explications fhould be fufficient for common ufe, and fince without fome attention to fuch demands the dictionary cannot become generally valuable, I have determined to confult the beft writers for explanations real as well as verbal, and perhaps I may at laft have reafon to fay, after one of the augmenters of Furetier, that my book is more learned than its author.

In explaining the general and popular language, it feems neceffary to fort the feveral fenfes of each word, and to exhibit firft its natural and primitive fignification, as

To

To *arrive*, to reach the fhore in a voyage.
He *arrived* at a fafe harbour

THEN to give its confequential meaning, *to
arrive*, to reach any place whether by land or
fea , as, he *arrived* at his country feat.

THEN its metaphorical fenfe, to obtain any
thing defired , as, he *arrived* at a peerage.

THEN to mention any obfervation that arifes
from the comparifon of one meaning with another; as, it may be remarked of the word
arrive, that in confequence of its original and
etymological fenfe, it cannot be properly applied but to words fignifying fomething de-
firable ; thus, we fay a man *arrived* at happi-
nefs, but cannot fay, without a mixture of
irony, he *arrived* at mifery

Ground, the earth, generally as oppofed to
the air or water. He fwam till he reached
ground. The bird fell to the *ground*.

THEN follows the accidental or confequential fignification, in which *ground* implies any
thing that lies under another , as, he laid co-
lours upon a rough *ground* The filk had blue
flowers on a red *ground*.

THEN

THEN the remoter or metaphorical fignifi-cation; as, the *ground* of his opinion was a falfe computation. The *ground* of his work was his father's manufcript.

AFTER having gone through the natural and figurative fenfes, it will be proper to fub-join the poetical fenfe of each word, where it differs from that which is in common ufe , as, *wanton* applied to any thing of which the mo-tion is irregular without terror, as

In *wanton* ringlets curl'd her hair.

To the poetical fenfe may fucceed the familiar; as of *toaft*, ufed to imply the perfon whofe health is drunk.

The wife man's 'paffion, and the vain man's
        toaft.   POPE.

THE familiar may be followed by the bur-lefque, as of *mellow*, applied to good fellow-fhip.

In all thy humours whether grave, or *mellow*.
                            ADDISON.

OR of *bite* ufed for *cheat*.

——More a dupe than wit,
Sappho can tell you, how this man was *bit*.
                            POPE.

D   AND

AND laftly, may be produced the peculiar fenfe, in which a word is found in any great author. As *faculties* in Shakefpeare fignifies the powers of authority.

——This Duncan
Has born his *faculties* fo meek, has been
So clear in his great office, that *&c.*

THE fignification of adjectives, may be often afcertained by uniting them to fubftantives, as *fimple fwain, fimple fheep*, fometimes the fenfe of a fubftantive may be elucidated by the epithets annexed to it in good authors, as the *boundlefs ocean*, the *open lawns*, and where fuch advantage can be gained by a fhort quotation it is not to be omitted.

THE difference of fignification in words generally accounted fynonimous, ought to be carefully obferved; as in *pride, haughtinefs, arrogance* and the ftrict and critical meaning ought to be diftinguifhed from that which is loofe and popular, as in the word *perfection*, which though in its philofophical and exact fenfe, it can be of little ufe among human beings, is often fo much degraded from its original fignification, that the academicians have inferted in their work *the perfection of a language*, and with a little more licentioufnefs
might

might have prevailed on themſelves to have added *the perfection of a dictionary.*

THERE are many other characters of words which it will be of uſe to mention. Some have both an active and paſſive ſignification, as *fearful*, that which gives or which feels terror, a *fearful prodigy*, a *fearful hare*. Some have a perſonal, ſome a real meaning, as in oppoſition to *old* we uſe the adjective *young* of animated beings, and *new* of other things. Some are reſtrained to the ſenſe of praiſe, and others to that of diſapprobation, ſo common-ly, though not always, we *exhort* to good actions, we *inſtigate* to ill, we *animate, incite* and *encourage* indifferently to good or bad So we uſually *aſcribe* good, but *impute* evil, yet neither the uſe of theſe words, nor per-haps of any other in our licentious language, is ſo eſtabliſhed as not to be often reverſed by the correcteſt writers. I ſhall therefore, ſince the rules of ſtile, like thoſe of law, ariſe from precedents often repeated, collect the teſtimo-nies on both ſides, and endeavour to diſcover and promulgate the decrees of cuſtom, who has ſo long poſſeſſed, whether by right or by uſurpation, the ſovereignty of words.

IT is neceſſary likewiſe to explain many words by their oppoſition to others; for con-

traries

traries are beſt ſeen when they ſtand together.
Thus the verb *ſtand* has one ſenſe as oppoſed
to *fall*, and another as oppoſed to *fly*, for
want of attending to which diſtinction, obvious as it is, the learned Dr. Bentley has ſquan-
dered his criticiſm to no purpoſe, on theſe
lines of Paradiſe Loſt.

——In heaps
Chariot and charioteer lay over-turn'd,
And fiery foaming ſteeds. What *ſtood, recoil'd*,
O'erwearied, through the faint Satanic hoſt,
Defenſive ſcarce, or with pale fear ſurpris'd
Fled ignominious——

" Here," ſays the critic, " as the ſentence is
" now read, we find that what *ſtood, fled*,"
and therefore he propoſes an alteration, which
he might have ſpared if he had conſulted a
dictionary, and found that nothing more was
affirmed than that thoſe *fled* who did *not*
fall

In explaining ſuch meanings as ſeem accidental and adventitious, I ſhall endeavour to
give an account of the means by which they
were introduced. Thus to *eke out* any thing, ſig-
nifies to lengthen it beyond its juſt dimenſions
by ſome low artifice, becauſe the work *eke* was
the uſual refuge of our old writers when they
wanted a ſyllable. And *buxom*, which means
only

only *obedient*, is now made, in familiar phrafes, to ftand foɪ *wanton*, becaufe ɪn an antɪent foɪm of marrɪage, before the reformatɪon, the bride promɪfed complaɪfance and obedɪence ɪn thefe terms, " I wɪll be bonair and *buxom* in bed and at board."

I ᴋɴᴏw well, my Lord, how triﬂing many of thefe ɪemarks wɪll appear feparately con-ﬁdered, and how eaﬁly they may give occa-ﬁon to the contemptuous merrɪment of fpoɪ-tɪve idlenefs, and the gloomy cenfures of aɪ-rogant ftupidɪty, but dulnefs it ɪs eafy to de-fpɪfe, and laughter ɪt is eafy to repay I ſhall not be follɪcɪtous what ɪs thought of my woɪk by fuch as know not the dɪfficulty oɪ impor-tance of phɪlologɪcal ftudɪes, nor ſhall thɪnk thofe that have done nothɪng qualɪfied to con-demn me for doɪng lɪttle It may not, how-eveɪ, be ɪmproper to remind them, that no terreftɪɪal greatnefs is more than an aggregate of little thɪngs, and to ɪnculcate after the Arabɪan proveɪb, that drops added to dropꜱ conftɪtute the ocean.

Tʜᴇʀᴇ remains yet to be conﬁdered the Dɪsᴛʀɪʙᴜᴛɪᴏɴ of woɪds into theɪr pɪopeɪ claſſes, or that paɪt of lexicography whɪch ɪs ftrɪ̈ctly crɪtɪcal.

Tʜᴇ

THE popular part of the language, which includes all words not appropriated to particular fciences, admits of many diftinctions and fubdivifions, as, into words of general ufe; words employed chiefly in poetry; words obfolete; words which are admitted only by particular writers, yet not in themfelves improper; words ufed only in burlefque writing, and words impure and barbarous

WORDS of general ufe will be known by having no fign of particularity, and their various fenfes will be fupported by authorities of all ages.

THE words appropriated to poetry will be diftinguifhed by fome mark prefixed, or will be known by having no authorities but thofe of poets.

OF antiquated or obfolete words, none will be inferted but fuch as are to be found in authors who wrote fince the acceffion of Elizabeth, from which we date the golden age of our language, and of thefe many might be omitted, but that the reader may require, with an appearance of reafon, that no difficulty fhould be left unrefolved in books which he finds himfelf invited to read, as confeffed and eftablifhed models of ftile. Thefe will

be

be likewife pointed out by fome note of ex-
clufion, but not of difgrace.

THE words which are found only in particular books, will be known by the fingle
name of him that has ufed them, but fuch
will be omitted, unlefs either their propriety,
elegance, or force, or the reputation of their
authors affords fome extraordinary reafon for
their reception.

WORDS ufed in burlefque and familiar com-
pofitions, will be likewife mentioned with
their proper authorities, fuch as *dudgeon* from
Butler, and *leafing* from Prior, and will be
diligently characterifed by marks of diftinction.

BARBAROUS or impure words and expref-
fions, may be branded with fome note of in-
famy, as they are carefully to be eradicated
wherever they are found, and they occur too
frequently even in the beft writers As in
Pope,

———*in* endlefs error *hurl'd.*

'*Tis thefe* that early taint the female foul.

In Addifon,

Attend to what a *leffer* mufe indites.

And

And in Dryden,

A dreadful quiet felt, and *worſer* far
Than arms——

If this part of the work can be well performed, it will be equivalent to the propoſal made by Boileau to the academicians, that they ſhould review all their polite writers, and correct ſuch impurities as might be found in them, that their authority might not contribute, at any diſtant time, to the depravation of the language.

WITH regard to queſtions of purity, or propriety, I was once in doubt whether I ſhould not attribute too much to myſelf in attempting to decide them, and whether my province was to extend beyond the propoſition of the queſtion, and the diſplay of the ſuffrages on each ſide, but I have been ſince determined by your Lordſhip's opinion, to interpoſe my own judgment, and ſhall therefore endeavour to ſupport what appears to me moſt conſonant to grammar and reaſon. Auſonius thought that modeſty forbad him to plead inability for a taſk to which Cæſar had judged him equal.

Cur me poſſe negem poſſe quod ille putat?

5   And

And I may hope, my Lord, that fince you, whofe authority in our language is fo gene-rally acknowledged, have commiffioned me to declare my own opinion, I fhall be confidered as exeicifing a kind of vicarious juiifdiction, and that the power which might have been denied to my own claim, will be readily allowed me as the delegate of your Lordfhip.

In citing authorities, on which the credit of every part of this work muft depend, it will be proper to obferve fome obvious rules, fuch as of preferring writers of the firft reputation to thofe of an inferior rank, of noting the quotations with accuracy, and of felecting, when it can be conveniently done, fuch fentences, as, befides their immediate ufe, may give pleafure or inftruction by conveying fome elegance of language, or fome precept of prudence, or piety.

It has been afked, on fome occafions, who fhall judge the judges? And fince with regard to this defign, a queftion may arife by what authority the authorities are felected, it is neceffary to obviate it, by declaring that many of the writers whofe teftimonies will be alledged, were felected by Mr. Pope, of whom I may be juftified in affirming, that were he ftill alive, folicitous as he was for the fuccefs

E   of

of this work, he would not be difpleafed that I have undertaken it

IT will be propei that the quotations be ranged accoiding to the ages of their authors, and it will affoid an agieeable amufement, if to the woids and phrafes which aie not of our own giowth, the name of the writer who firft intioduced them can be affixed, and if, to woids which are now antiquated, the autho-rity be fubjoined of him who laft admitted them. Thus foi *fcathe* and *buxom*, now ob-folete, Milton may be cited.

———The mountain oak
Stands *fcath'd* to heaven———
———He with bioad fails
Winnow'd the *buxom* air———

By this method every woid will have its hiftory, and the reader will be informed of the giadual changes of the language, and have before his eyes the iife of fome words, and the fall of others. But obfervations fo minute and accuiate are to be defired rather than expected, and if ufe be carefully fupplied, curiofity muft fometimes bear its difappoint-ments.

THIS, my Lord, is my idea of an Englifh dictionary, a dictionary by which the pro-
nun-

nunciation of our language may be fixed, and its attainment facilitated, by which its purity may be preserved, its use afcertained, and its duration lengthened. And though, perhaps, to correct the language of nations by books of grammar, and amend their manners by difcourfes of morality, may be tafks equally difficult, yet as it is unavoidable to wifh, it is natural likewife to hope, that your Lordfhip's patronage may not be wholly loft, that it may contribute. to the prefervation of antient, and the improvement of modern writers; that it may promote the reformation of thofe tranflators, who for want of underftanding the characteriftical diffeience of tongues, have formed a chaotic dialect of hetcrogeneous phrafes, and awaken to the care of purer diction, fome men of genius, whofe attention to argument makes them negligent of ftile, or whofe rapid imagination, like the Peruvian torrents, when it brings down gold, mingles it with fand.

WHEN I furvey the Plan which I have laid before you, I cannot, my Lord, but confefs, that I am frighted at its extent, and, like the foldiers of Cæfar, look on Britain as a new world, which it is almoft madnefs to invade. But I hope, that though I fhould not complete the conqueft, I fhall at leaft difcover the

the coaft, civilize part of the inhabitants, and make it eafy for fome other adventurer to proceed farther, to reduce them wholly to fubjection, and fettle them under laws.

WE are taught by the great Roman orator, that every man fhould propofe to himfelf the higheft degree of excellence, but that he may ftop with honour at the fecond or third: though therefore my performance fhould fall below the excellence of other dictionaries, I may obtain, at leaft, the praife of having endeavoured well, nor fhall I think it any reproach to my diligence, that I have retired without a triumph from a conteft with united academies and long fucceffions of learned compilers. I cannot hope in the warmeft moments, to preferve fo much caution through fo long a work, as not often to fink into negligence, or to obtain fo much knowledge of all its parts, as not frequently to fail by ignorance. I expect that fometimes the defire of accuracy will urge me to fuperfluities, and fometimes the fear of prolixity betray me to omiffions; that in the extent of fuch variety I fhall be often bewildred, and in the mazes of fuch intricacy be frequently entangled; that in one part refinement will be fubtilifed beyond exactnefs, and evidence dilated in another beyond perfpicuity. Yet I

do

do not defpair of approbation from thofe who knowing the uncertainty of conjecture, the fcantinefs of knowledge, the fallibility of memory, and the unfteadinefs of attention, can compare the caufes of error with the means of avoiding it, and the extent of art with the capacity of man; and whatever be the event of my endeavours, I fhall not eafily regret an attempt which has procured me the honour of appearing thus publickly,

My Lord,

> *Your Lordfhip's*
>
> *Moft Obedient*
>
> *and*
>
> *Moft Humble Servant,*

S A M. J O H N S O N.

Lightning Source UK Ltd.
Milton Keynes UK
UKHW020947110821
388657UK00010B/129